The Prophet's Personality

peace be upon him

MUHAMMAD ABDULRAOOF

Contents

With Himself 6

With his Family 7

Muhammad the Messenger, the Man of Right and Justice 9

Muhammad the Messenger, the Man of Good Morals 11

Muhammad the Prophet, the Man of Science and Civilization .. 12

Muhammad the Messenger, the Man of Permissiveness 14

Muhammad the Messenger, the Man of Religion and 16
Government

Muhammad the Messenger, the Man of Cleanness and 17
Environmental Care

Muhammad the Messenger; the Man of Elegance and Beauty ... 18

Smiling was the Prophet›s Motto 19

Muhammad the Messenger, the Man of Tolerance & 20
Noble Forgiveness

Muhammad the Messenger; the Tender Hearted Companion ... 21

Muhammad the Messenger Encourages Noble 23
& Refined Sports

Muhammad the Messenger; the Builder of the 24
Distinguished Structural

Muhammad the Messenger; the Man of Education 25

Muhammad dealing with People in War (the Noble Warrior)..... 27

Exploring the Character of Prophet Muhammad 30

With Himself

The Prophet was a great man; he built up this greatness through his confidence and steadiness on his principles. He was of good manners and fair deeds with all people; enemies and friends. In addition to that, modesty and flexibility were of his great qualities away from complexity and arrogance.

- He was frank with himself and satisfied with his principles. He had specific targets and a clear vision.

-He held on his principles till he conveyed his divine message spreading all his noble principles which are not known by those who hate and vilify him.

- He owned all the good qualities of a person gained by innate and all the characteristics of human perfection wished by the wise.

- Handsome features are mixed with noble manners and wise mentality to form a teacher who awakened the world like the sun enlightening darkness. He gave live to all human beings after being buried for ages and ages under ignorance and selfishness.

With his Family

The observer of the private life of Muhammad the Messenger, will admire the man who came from a harsh desert environment prevailed by ignorance and anarchism, and wonder "how could he reach the highest levels of incomparable family success?"

Muhammad (PBUH) was an inexhaustible stream of love, warmth, tenderness, sensitivity and emotions.

He was the perfect lover to his family and wives. He was playing and joking with them. He was giving them love and tenderness; for example, he was expressing gently his love to his wife Aisha by intending to drink from the same cup she drank from putting his lips on the place from which she drank sending a secret message warming up her heart and feelings. This was just one example from many in his life.

He even represented the loyal lover in a happy family. He did not forget his dead wife khadeeja, but he kept remembering her favors by having good relations with her relatives. He was very angry when khadeeja was disparged in his presence. Abu najeeh narrated in the story of Hala –khadiga's sister- when Hala asked for permission to meet the Messenger, Aisha said" Allah gave you the young wife instead of the old one-she means khadiga-". So the Messenger became very angry till she said" I swear I wont mention her after now except in a good way".

In spite of Muhammad's heavy burdens as being the chief of the Islamic state, the commander of the army and the moral and intellectual guidance to his followers, he did not forget his duties towards his family by helping them in the housework, showing that woman has a great value in Islam.

Al Aswad reported that he asked Aisha (the Prophet's wife) about what the Messenger had been doing in his house. She replied that he was serving his family and when the time came to pray he left to prayer.(Narrated by Al Bukhari)

Muhammad the Messenger, the Man of Right and Justice

He loved right and justice and ruled according to this. He did not fear to be blamed because of applying justice. He did not flatter any one for his rank, money or his pedigree, in the contrary, he supported the weak and stand against the strong in giving them their rights back.

He was so fair and stick to the right to the extend that he did not flatter even the dearest people to him. It happened that an eminent woman from the Family of Mekhzoum- (a great family in Makkah at that time)- stole, so she deserved a punishment for her crime. Her family went to one of the Prophet's followers - he was the dearest to him- to ask the Prophet for forgiveness. When Muhammad (PBUH) listened to the request of his dearest friend to forgive this woman, he became very angry because of breaking and infracting the holiness of justice after he had become a Muslim.

Aisha said that Quraish was very concerned about the woman of the family of Makhzoum who had stolen so they thought that no one dare to speak with the Messenger in this case except Osama bin Zeid, the dearest to the Messenger. Osama talked to the Messenger, who had replied: "do you mediate in one of Allah's laws? Then he stood and gave a speech telling the people that the nations living before them were destroyed because they didn't punish the eminent but did only punish the weak when committing any crime. And he swore if his daughter Fatima stole, he would punish her.

Muhammad the Messenger, the Man of Noble Manners

The most remarkable thing in Muhammad is his gentle and exalted manners with all people; his friends and his enemies. This is witnessed by all the just men.

He was a man of good reception, the smile never left his face, his words were sweet, he acted in a mannered way even towards those offending him, and ignored interfering in trivial things.

He taught his followers that the best of people is the best mannered.

He also taught his followers that the closest one to him in Paradise is the one who has the best manners.

The good manners of Muhammad the Messenger were not towards his followers only but also towards his enemies; when the Prophet were asked to curse upon his enemies he refused, saying:" I'm not sent by Allah to curse but I'm the mercy sent to the whole world".(narrated by Muslim)

Muhammad the Messenger, the Man of Good Morals

The most remarkable thing in Muhammad is his gentle and exalted manners with all people; his friends and his enemies. This is witnessed by all the just men.

He was a man of good reception, the smile never left his face, his words were sweet, he acted in a mannered way even towards those offending him, and ignored interfering in trivial things.

He taught his followers that the best of people is the best mannered.

He also taught his followers that the closest one to him in Paradise is the one who has the best manners.

The good manners of Muhammad the Messenger were not towards his followers only but also towards his enemies; when the Prophet were asked to curse upon his enemies he refused, saying:"

I'm not sent by Allah to curse but I'm the mercy sent to the whole world".(narrated by Muslim).

Muhammad the Prophet, the Man of Science and Civilization

Again another unjust, quick verdict has been set upon the Prophet that he is against science and civilization, but this in fact may be because of the status of the Muslims now days that causes that verdict against Muhammad (PBUH) and Islam.

An honest researcher-if applying the ethics of the scientific research- can not but addict that Muhammad had built for his followers the basics of science and the way of civilization that was the reason behind the strong nation that they've established and spread its science, civilization principles and ethics to the whole world; the world that witness what the Islamic civilization in Andalusia offered Europe and humanity in their scientific revolution.

How couldn't he be a man of science and civilization while the first word he received from the Almighty Allah written in the holy Quran was the order to "READ"?

Plus there is a chapter in the holy Quran named (the pen) as being the first science tool and the first created by Allah.

He is the man of an advanced civilization with fixed assets. No one except him (PBUH) was able to change an ignorant, violent and unmoral nation to a nation of ethics and leading the escort education and science.

Muhammad was able to find an exit for his nation from the dark, being-behind, oppression and aggression to the light and promotion. He built the civilization basics that balance between the needs of the soul and that of the body which helped his followers to lead the world for decades when they hung on these basics.

But what is happening now days to his followers in being behind in science and civilization is because of what the American and European colonization left behind.... Agents, in the Islamic world, controlling the reins of events to obstacle any literary movement depending on the civilization basics of Messenger Muhammad.

Muhammad the Messenger, the Man of Permissiveness

The evil propaganda and the false accusations, that don't have even the less degree of any scientific faithfulness, disfigured the reality of Muhammad because it imagined him as a leader who opposes permissiveness and dialogue. Muhammad (may Allah's blessing be upon him) is the caller of permissiveness in all parts of life which is witnessed by all his behaviors. Look at this example: some Jews were praying for his death while they delude him that they were welcoming him. They were telling him (Alsaam alaikom) which means "death be upon you" instead of (Alsalam alaikom) which means "peace be upon you"…Only the letter "L" differs!!!!

Although the prophet knew their bad intention, his forgiveness were very surprising for every equitable.

Imagine yourself in this situation, what will be your reaction? Then you will know the reaction of the Prophet…

Imagine yourself a leader or a ruler being obeyed hearing a man asking Allah for your death with deceiving words that may be understood as good. May be you forgive him in his praying for your death but you can't forgive his deceit.

Now dear reader; be just when you read the reaction made by Prophet Muhammad concerning this rousing scene and be a fair referee.

One day the Prophet (PBUH) was sitting with his wife Aisha

when some Jews passed by and pretended to say hi to him while they meant to insult him but his beloved wife understood their deceiving way of their words and replied with the same insulting words.

Now the question is: did the Prophet get satisfied with this action?

The answer is No, on the contrary he blamed his beloved wife and ordered her to be more lenient and gentle and never be violent or harsh.

Aisha said: "The Jews were greeting the Prophet (Allah's blessing may be upon him) saying (Alsaam alikom) which means "death be upon you" so she replied: death and curse be upon you. But the Prophet (Allah's blessing may be upon him) said: wait Aisha, Allah loves the kindness in the whole situation".

Muhammad the Messenger, the Man of Cleanness and Environmental Care

One of the special features of the Prophet's life and religion is his strict teachings dictated to his followers which forced them to give great concern to neatness and protecting the environment.

So the Prophet ordered his followers to wash their different body parts that are exposed to pollution as the face, mouth, nose, hands and feet five times per day or more, and washing the whole body frequently as much as possible.

-He warned people not to pollute the areas near living places with dirt.

-He insisted on the importance of getting rid of any dirt caused by humans.

-He obliged his followers to clean their clothes from dirt " najass ".

-He taught his followers "medical isolation"; so he ordered them not to enter the places affected with epidemic diseases and not to leave it in order to prevent the spread of diseases.

With these instructions and many others, the Prophet (PBUH) built a complete social system within a healthy atmosphere and clean environment. So there is no place in the Prophet's teachings for pollution, dirtiness in clothing, body and the whole environment.

Muhammad the Messenger, the Man of Cleanness and Environmental Care

One of the special features of the Prophet's life and religion is his strict teachings dictated to his followers which forced them to give great concern to neatness and protecting the environment.

So the Prophet ordered his followers to wash their different body parts that are exposed to pollution as the face, mouth, nose, hands and feet five times per day or more, and washing the whole body frequently as much as possible.

-He warned people not to pollute the areas near living places with dirt.

-He insisted on the importance of getting rid of any dirt caused by humans.

-He obliged his followers to clean their clothes from dirt " najass ".

-He taught his followers "medical isolation"; so he ordered them not to enter the places affected with epidemic diseases and not to leave it in order to prevent the spread of diseases.

With these instructions and many others, the Prophet (PBUH) built a complete social system within a healthy atmosphere and clean environment. So there is no place in the Prophet's teachings for pollution, dirtiness in clothing, body and the whole environment.

Muhammad the Messenger; the Man of Elegance and Beauty

If you ask about the things that the Prophet like most, you will get three answers starting with perfume. He liked very much the nice smell of perfumes and never smelled bad. Moreover the Prophet was very elegant; he was the best looking ever among his people, shinning in his clothes like a moon in the sky.

And the great thing is that the Prophet's appearance was such of elegance in a society very far from classiness, cleanness and sophistication .He was as a beautiful flower in the arid desert, and like the warm fire in the frozen desert and like the spring in a lifeless earth.

Smiling was the Prophet›s Motto

How much important it is in such a world, full of social crises and psychological disease we live in, to keep a smile on our faces like the one the Prophet asked his followers to keep all the time.

The Prophet released his followers from all heart diseases, psychological crises and life pressures that demolish human life to reach happiness and inner peace. So he made the smile his slogan in sorrows and happiness and was never seen but smiling. His smile cured the sadness of all people around him and healed the pains of his companions.

Abdullah bin Al Hareth reported:" I never saw a man smiling more than the Prophet (PBUH)."

But he never went over the limits; he did not exaggerate in the way he smiled or laughed, he used to smile politely and respectfully.

Abdullah bin Al Hareth reported:" The Prophet's way to laugh was only by smiling." Narrated by Al Tarmithi

It means that he used to laugh without cackling and full of respect.

Muhammad the Messenger, the Man of Tolerance & Noble Forgiveness

Whoever browses the history of great men and leaders, during a victory after a lost battle, will find one common trait among them all, except for Prophets, which is revenge.

Muhammad the Messenger (PBUH) had given a superb example for the nobleness of the victorious. Despite being exiled from Makkah, his possessions being confiscated and being hurt badly by its people at the beginning of his prophecy, upon entering Makkah overwhelmingly victorious, his great personality & generosity would not give room for revenge. He had forgiven all those who have oppressed him while being able to exact severe vengeance on them.

He told them: "You can go for you are free"

In such a way Islam had raised Muhammad and his companions on such refined manners, free from the shackles of selfness & selfishness. For the Quran says: "Show forgiveness, enjoin what is good, and turn away from the foolish (i.e. don't punish them)."

Muhammad the Messenger; the Tender Hearted Companion

What will be your reaction towards someone declaiming against something you really love?

What if you were a religious man and someone came and desecrated the place of your worship rudely?

No doubt that you will rage and rush to exact punishment on him. Muhammad (PBUH) did not do so, for he did not believe in hasty reactions, he had complete control over his reactions by judging wisely before doing any action. The following story proves that he used to treat every incident with wide and far sighted intellect:

A Bedouin came from the desert who had no contact with the new city (Madinah) that Muhammad (PBUH) had erected among his companions in the new capital. This Bedouin acted in a very strange manner to the people of the civilized Madinah.

What was this action you think?

Indeed it was one of the strangest things a man can do, to urinate in a well respected and public place in front of everyone. That is what this man had done; he urinated in the mosque in front of Muhammad & his companions in the most sacred place to them. It was a horrible scene, the companions could not control themselves and they yelled at him to stop what he was doing. Even though such incident took only seconds, Muhammad's (PBUH) reactions did not precede his brain. During this split second he had analyzed the Bedouin character, which did such wrong act in the place of his worship and where he runs his state. His brain (PBUH) had showed him that this Bedouin is illiterate and his action holds no hostile intentions. It is a mere act of backwardness from the culture of cleanliness and decency that Muhammad (PBUH) had built in his capital. He ordered his companions to leave the Bedouin without scolding him. After the Bedouin had finished, Muhammad (PBUH) came up to him and informed him that he can not do such thing in this place. The Bedouin was so happy from Muhammad's (PBUH) way of teaching him and was taken by his manners and said "O Allah have mercy on me and Muhammad and no one else".

Muhammad the Messenger Encourages Noble & Refined Sports

Muhammad the Messenger (PBUH) had encouraged his companions to practice the refined sport that is based on strengthening the body and recreating the spirit and bringing benefit unto the society without wasting money and soul and without corrupting manners.

He himself had practiced some sports like running, wrestling & horseback ridding. The only condition to sport in Muhammad's (PBUH) constitution is to own noble and refined manners and to have sublime goals.

Muhammad the Messenger; the Builder of the Distinguished Structural

Muhammad (PBUH) had built in a barren desert a unique cultural system that was never known before. It was distinguished with the accuracy of planning and observing the interest of the city all in a beautiful & attractive view. The Mosque was in the center of the capital and it was the headquarters for running the city and the conference center for people during important events and emergencies. Such center (the mosque) was the refuge for the poor & needy, where the state and the charitable bodies provide for them food and shelter. Also it was the shelter for the strangers who come from outside the state where they find food and hostel.

The civilization system built by Muhammad (PBUH) depended on establishing markets & houses around the mosque to facilitate the transaction between people of the markets and those of the houses from one side and to facilitate their contact with the mosque from the other side. The people in the city of Muhammad (PBUH) are one entity always in contact; everyone is in the centre of the events with no discrimination or suppression.

Muhammad the Messenger; the Man of Education

he fair researcher would be wondering by the amazing ability that Mohammad the messenger owned, which made him capable of transferring a nation who don't know how to write and read into a nation which is proud of knowledge, and had scientists of very high levels in the state and society. And looking for the secret behind this success, the researcher will find out that the Almighty Allah gave Muhammad the messenger great educational abilities, being an eloquent speaker, a convincing lecturer and a successful educator.

What helped him through this success is perhaps his proficiency in the conversational methods, having the attention, and stimulating the mind to the information. These are the essential effects in Muhammad's educational teachings.

Notice this example when he asks his companions:"who is the insolvent?", then he waits for their answer even thought he knows that the answer will be wrong, but this is his intellectual conversation methods to stabilize the information. Then, as expected, his students say a wrong answer, he listens to them till they finish, then he gives them the right answer. Similar examples for this effective educational way are many in the teachings of Muhammad the messenger.

Muhammad's instructions that obligate all people whether males or females to learn and reach a specific educational level, then to encourage who wants to learn more had an effective role in the substantial leap that Muhammad created in the educational field.

Some of his instructions and teachings concerning this field: "seeking knowledge is an obligation upon each Muslim"; in Muhammad's speeches and in the revealed book-the Holy Quran- the word (Muslim) includes both males and females.

Muhammad dealing with People in War (the Noble Warrior)

1- his nobility towards the enemy soldiers inside the Battle:

Muhammad, having noble morals and applying the instructions of the holy Quran, had never betrayed anyone even if it was his enemy. He never broke an agreement with any one until the second party is the one to break it .In his Battles, whether he was the victorious or his enemy, he never torture the wounded and the captives of war, and he don't mutilate the dead bodies, and he used to prohibit his soldiers and army staff from doing that whatever the case may be.

He and his companions gave humanity marvelous examples for noble morals during wars.

2- His nobility towards women in battles :

Take this wondrous example that captives the mind and shakes the feelings.

In one of the decisive battles that Muhammad went through ,one of his military staff –his cousin Ali the son of Taleb- saw a veiled enemy soldier moving between the corpse of the wounded and the dead of Muhammad's army and started to mutilate them in a horrible way, and he went as far as maiming the body of (Hamza), Muhammad's uncle. This scene terrified him and he determined to take revenge from this soldier by killing him, immediately he went to him like a fast arrow ,but he was surprised (when he raised his sword to kill him) that this soldier is not but a woman disguised in a man's outfit.

Notice the wondrous scene and the great principles of Muhammad's soldiers; that during the moments he raised his sword to kill the offender, this leader balanced between revenge and high principles that he absorbed from Muhammad's school, so he lowered his sword and repressed his anger and released this woman despite her ugly deeds and actions against his friends.

What kind of morals is this? And what kind of principles? What kind of greatness? What kind of women respect and mercy even if being an enemy?

This is the greatness of Muhammad and his followers, and the greatness of Islam that taught them this.

3- His nobility towards the captives of war

Despite the covenants of human rights and the international agreements yet the captive of war still moan under the burden and the violence of the psychological and physical torturing, and the flagrant violation of human rights.

However from more than fourteen centuries, Muhammad the messenger legislated a great method and way for all the world of how to treat a war captive, which, if humanity had applied, will find a way out of the captives' crisis in this confused world. This crisis is still shocking the feelings of everyone owning a living conscience and noble morals. That is because Muhammad had prevented the violation of human rights absolutely no matter what the justification was.

So it's not acceptable neither to torture the captive physically or psychologically nor to curse, swear or even keep food and drinks away from him. In the contrary, Muhammad and his companions went to the point where they gave priority to the captives in their food and drinks.

This scene was described and praised by a Quranic verse:" And they give food to the poor, the orphan and the captive, for love of Allah ".

You judge now these great behaviors of Muhammad and his companions towards the captives.

The captives nowadays need, in deed, to live in the world of Muhammad to be treated the same way as Muhammad did with his captives, with mercy and respecting their humanity that was taken by the means of the weapons of mass destruction and dirty wars under unlawful names.

As a conclusion we have to say, that Muhammad has to be proud of his ideal city that is more developed than the cities of the whole world in this age. He is in deed the pioneer in all fields of live practically not only in terms of commercials and banners. Find just one case, if you can, in which Muhammad or his followers tortured their captives physically or psychologically…….

Exploring the Character of Prophet Muhammad

Almighty Allah says:

[Certainly you have in the Messenger of Allah an excellent exemplar for those who hope in Allah and the latter day and remember Allah much](Al-Ahzab 33:21)

We will try to explore some unique aspects of the character and biography of the Prophet (peace and blessings be upon him). In doing so, let's sincerely pray that many of us will start a process of change to acquire many of these traits of our beloved Prophet and apply them, in sha` Allah.

In 610 CE, Prophet Muhammad, the last and the seal of all Prophets (peace and blessings be upon them all), began receiving the revelation.

Almighty Allah says:

[Muhammad is not the father of any man among you, but he is the Messenger of Allah and the seal of the Prophets, and Allah is Ever-Aware of all things.] (Al-Ahzab 33:40)

Muhammad (peace and blessings be upon him) provided a model of how people should live as individuals and as members of the society. The truths revealed to and taught by him stress that this world did not spring up by itself but was created by One God (Allah), Who continues to watch over it. All human beings are Allah's servants and are accountable before Him for their actions. Death is not the end of humans' life; rather it is the beginning of another eternal world, where the righteous will enjoy the bliss of Paradise and the wicked will dwell in raging Hellfire.

Prophet Muhammad (peace and blessings be upon him) changed the tide of the human history and captured the imagination of the world by Allah's will. He taught a religion that is based on:

1- Worshipping One Immortal God (Almighty Allah)

2- Believing in reality, not superstition

3- Teaching the humans to utilize nature (instead of worshipping it), thus paving the way for the scientific era

4- Giving political power to the people and not hereditarily keeping it in the hands of one monarch or chieftain

5- Showing the people all over the world — through the example of the Prophet — how to live, cooperate, and work in an atmosphere of justice and peace, not cruelty and oppression

6- Teaching that if one always fears to displease Almighty Allah, then there shouldn't be anything else that one should fear

7- Teaching that if one rises above negative impulses and pessimism, one can overcome all enemies, and if one sacrifices this world for the next, one will eventually have the best of both worlds

His Mission

Prophet Muhammad (peace and blessings be upon him) was entrusted, for more than 23 years, with propagating Allah's words and message to the humanity. It was this role that brought him to a collision with his people. He was inflicted with all forms of adversity, from the pain of hunger to the trepidation of battle. Yet, throughout the 23 years of his mission, the Prophet always remained just and steadfast in his actions. His conduct was governed by a fear of displeasing Allah. During this mission, he changed the history of Arabia and laid the foundations of a permanent change in the world's history.

Within 100 years, this religious revolution caused the decline and then defeat of the Persian, Sassanid, and Byzantine Empires. Islam swept through:

1- Iraq and Iran to Bukhara, Uzbekistan, in the east

2- Syria and Palestine to Egypt and then North Africa in the west

Contrary to the claims we hear today, the divinely revealed message of Islam came with the objective of reviving and confirming Allah's religions of Islam, which were revealed to Abraham and his offspring, Ishmael and Isaac, and their descendents, including Moses (Judaism) and Jesus (Christianity).

This noble religion, whose book is surely preserved by Almighty Allah Himself for eternity, has opened new, unexplored opportunities for the human race. It brought the age of democracy and freedom of speech to the world. It also helped make new discoveries in the world of science by encouraging the humans to use their most valuable gift — the mind or intellect. Islam encourages the human race to seek religious truth and to explore the scientific phenomena to raise the standard and quality of life. A big question arises: How could the Prophet and his well-taught and faithful Companions spread Islam in a very few years and with very little human losses? Let's look at the Prophet's character so that we might all be able to learn from this good exemplar.

His Exemplary Conduct

Prophet Muhammad had a perfectly balanced personality. He was patient, truthful, and magnanimous. He presented the highest example of human nobility. He disciplined himself by staying aloof from quarrels and quibbles. He never engaged in foul utterances or abuse. Even before prophethood, he was called as-sadiq al-amin (the truthful and trustworthy).

He had every opportunity to live a comfortable life and even become the king of Arabia. But, he refused all this for the sake of establishing the new world order of Islam in pursuit of truth.

Time occupies an important place in the teachings of the Prophet (peace and blessings be upon him). The Companions (may Allah be pleased with them all) were taught in the Prophetic school. They used to divide their time in the following way:

1- A portion for worshipping Almighty Allah

2- A portion for self-examination

3- A portion for reflection over the mysteries of creation

4- A portion for eating, drinking, and enjoying social life
Let's visit some stories from the biography of Prophet Muhammad, so as to get acquainted with some of his sublime manners.

Prophet Muhammad (peace and blessings be upon him) lived among others as an equal. No bitter criticism or provocation would make him lose his composure, and no praise could make him vain. He lived in such taqwa (piety and fear of Allah) that he was always an example of modesty and leniency. He spoke little. He walked in a way that suggested his reverence of and humbleness before Almighty Allah. Criticism never angered him. He would assert that he is Allah's servant and would act as befits a servant of Allah.

He was so keen to assert the difference between him as a human prophet and Almighty Allah as the Omnipotent Creator. Once, a Companion said, "If it is the will of Allah and the will of the Prophet." The Prophet (peace and blessings be upon him) showed his disapproval of this and said:

"Are you trying to equate me with Allah? Rather, one should say, 'If Allah alone wills."(Ahmad)

Toward the end of the Prophet's life, his Egyptian wife, Mariyah Al-Qibtiyah, gave birth to a beautiful child, Ibrahim, around the end of the 8th year of Hijrah. Ibrahim died in the 10th year of Hijrah (632 CE) when he was still one year and a half. The Prophet (peace and blessings be upon him) wept the death of his son. In his deepest grief, he uttered these words:

"Allah knows, Ibrahim, how far we feel sorrowful for your departure. The eyes tear and the heart grieves, but we will say nothing except what pleases Allah."(Al-Bukhari)

The death of Ibrahim coincided with a solar eclipse. People from ancient times believed that solar and lunar eclipses might be caused by the death of some important person. The people of Madinah began attributing the eclipse to the death of the Prophet's son, Ibrahim. Greatly displeased by this, the Prophet (peace and blessings be upon him) gathered the people and addressed them, saying:

"Eclipses of the sun and the moon are not caused by the death of any human being; they are two of Allah's signs. When you see the eclipse, you should show gratefulness to Almighty Allah and offer prayer to Him."(Al-Bukhari)

On one of the journeys of the Prophet, the group of travelers embarked on roasting a goat. One volunteered to slaughter the animal, another to skin it, and another to cook it. The Prophet (peace and blessings be upon him) said that he would collect the firewood. Although his Companions were quite ready to do all the work, the Prophet wanted to help and participate in the teamwork. He never assumed superiority over his Companions.

Three years after the Hijrah to Madinah, the Makkan opponents mounted an assault against the newly emerging Muslim community, and the battle of Uhud took place. The Muslims initially had the upper hand till some mistakes were committed in the battlefield that caused the Makkans to attack the Muslims from the rear. The Prophet was left alone, encircled by the armed forces of the enemy; they advanced toward him, and the Prophet started calling out his Companions.

Once a disbeliever from the Makkans, threw a stone at the Prophet and injured his face. This caused the Prophet (peace and blessings be upon him) to bleed profusely and to fall down. When the Companions found him in this state, he said, "How can those who tinged the face of their Prophet (i.e. wounded him in the face), who calls them to their Lord, ever succeed (in the hereafter)?" (Ibn `Asakir)

Even with this light objection, Jibreel (Angel Gabriel) was ordered by Almighty Allah to descend down with the following Qur'anic verse:

[It is no concern at all of you (Muhammad) whether He (Allah) relent toward them or punish them, for they are evildoers.](Aal `Imran 3:128)

Acting upon this verse, the Prophet (peace and blessings be upon him), as related by `Abdullah ibn Mas`ud, would say the following supplication: "My Lord, forgive my people, for they know not what they do." (Ibn Hisham)

www.ingramcontent.com/pod-product-compliance
Lightning Source LLC
LaVergne TN
LVHW021050100526
838202LV00082B/5425